D0118795

The Earth Is the Lord's

THE EARTH IS THE LORD'S

Kathryn M. Patton, Editor

Photographs by William H. Johnson

The earth is the LORD's, and the fulness thereof;
the world, and they that dwell therein.

PSALM 24:1

IDEALS PUBLICATIONS
NASHVILLE, TENNESSEE

ISBN 0-8249-5883-7

Published by Ideals Publications
A division of Guideposts
535 Metroplex Drive, Suite 250
Nashville, Tennessee 37211
www.idealsbooks.com

Copyright © 2005 by Ideals Publications

All rights reserved. No part of this publication may be reproduced or transmitted in any form or by any means, electronic or mechanical, including photocopy, recording, or any information storage and retrieval system, without permission in writing from the publisher.

Color separations by Precision Color Graphics, Franklin, Wisconsin

Printed and bound in the U.S.A. by RR Donnelley

Library of Congress Cataloging-in-Publication Data

The Earth is the Lord's / edited by Kathryn M. Patton.
        p. cm.
    Includes index.
    ISBN 0-8249-5883-7 (alk. paper)
    I. Nature—Religious aspects—Christianity. I. Patton, Kathryn.
    BT695.5.E268 2004
    231.7'65—dc22

                                    2004026036

10 9 8 7 6 5 4 3 2 1

Publisher, Patricia A. Pingry
Book Editor, Kelly Riley Baugh
Art Director, Eve DeGrie
Copy Editor, Melinda Rathjen
Permissions Editor, Patsy Jay

Book Design by Eve DeGrie

ACKNOWLEDGMENTS
DAVIS, KATHERINE K. "Let All Things Now Living," copyright © 1939, 1966 by E. C. Schirmer Music Company, a division of ECS Publishing, Boston, MA. Used by permission. TORRANS, DICK. Music for "All Things Bright and Beautiful," copyright © 2004 by Melode Inc. All rights reserved. Used by permission. Words by Cecil Frances Alexander.

Cover photograph: Under a brilliant blue sky, the sandstone formations rise from the earth at Arches National Park in Utah.

Page two photograph: Golden-hued sugar maples herald the arrival of autumn.

TABLE OF CONTENTS

The Beauty of the Earth

Chapter 1

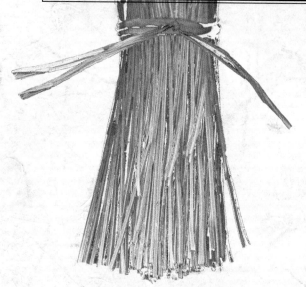

Arrowleaf balsamroot adorns the
banks of the Snake River, alongside
the majesty of the Grand Tetons.

O sing unto the LORD a new song:

sing unto the LORD, all the earth. Sing unto the LORD,

bless his name; shew forth his salvation from day to day.

Declare his glory among the heathen, his wonders among all people.

For the LORD is great, and greatly to be praised:

he is to be feared above all gods. For all the gods of the nations are idols:

but the LORD made the heavens. Honour and majesty are before him:

strength and beauty are in his sanctuary. Give unto the LORD,

O ye kindreds of the people, give unto the LORD glory and strength.

Let the heavens rejoice, and let the earth be glad;

let the sea roar, and the fulness thereof. Let the field be joyful,

and all that is therein: then shall all the trees of the wood rejoice

Before the LORD: for he cometh, for he cometh to judge the earth:

he shall judge the world with righteousness, and the people with his truth.

PSALM 96:1-7, 11-13

Otter Cove, in Maine's Acadia
National Park, reflects the wonder
of Cadillac Mountain.

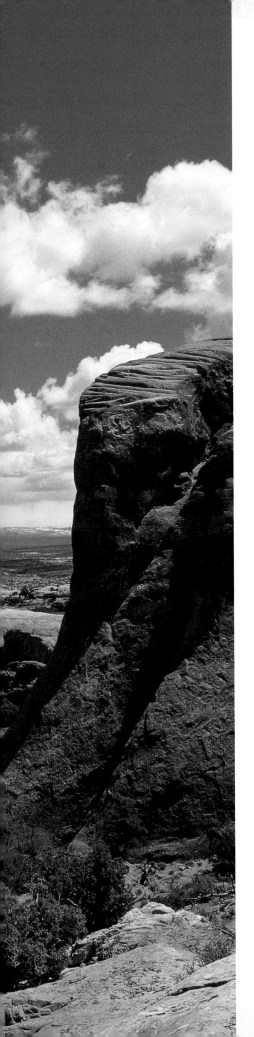

Drop down, ye heavens, from above,

and let the skies pour down righteousness:

let the earth open, and let them bring forth salvation,

and let righteousness spring up together;

I the LORD have created it.

For thus saith the LORD that created the heavens;

God himself that formed the earth and made it;

he hath established it, he created it not in vain,

he formed it to be inhabited:

I am the LORD; and there is none else.

ISAIAH 45:8,18

Sandstone formations rise
to the heavens at Arches
National Park in Utah.

Praise ye the LORD. Praise ye the LORD from the heavens: praise him in the heights. Praise ye him, all his angels: praise ye him, all his hosts.

Praise ye him, sun and moon: praise him, all ye stars of light. Praise him,

ye heavens of heavens, and ye waters that be above the heavens.

Let them praise the name of the LORD: for he commanded, and they were created.

He hath also stablished them for ever and ever: he hath made a decree

which shall not pass. Praise the LORD from the earth, ye dragons, and all deeps:

Fire, and hail; snow, and vapours; stormy wind fulfilling his word:

Mountains, and all hills; fruitful trees, and all cedars: Beasts, and all cattle;

creeping things, and flying fowl: Kings of the earth, and all people;

princes, and all judges of the earth: Both young men, and maidens;

old men, and children: Let them praise the name of the LORD:

for his name alone is excellent; his glory is above the earth and heaven.

He also exalteth the horn of his people, the praise of all his saints;

even of the children of Israel, a people near unto him. Praise ye the LORD.

PSALM 148

Blooming apple trees grace the banks of
the Merrimack River in Massachusetts.

For the Beauty of the Earth

Folliott S. Pierpoint

Conrad Kocher

1. For the beau – ty of the earth, For the glo – ry
2. For the beau – ty of each hour Of the day and

of the skies, For the love which from our birth
of the night, Hill and vale, and tree, and flow'r,

o – ver and a – round us lies; Lord of all, to
sun and moon, and stars of light, Lord of all, to

thee we raise This our hymn of grate – ful praise.
thee we raise This our hymn of grate – ful praise.

For the joy of human love,

Brother, sister, parent, child,

Friends on earth, and friends above,

For all gentle thoughts and mild,

Lord of all, to thee we raise

This our hymn of grateful praise.

For thy Church that evermore

Lifteth holy hands above,

Off'ring upon ev'ry shore

Her pure sacrifice of love,

Lord of all, to thee we raise

This our hymn of grateful praise.

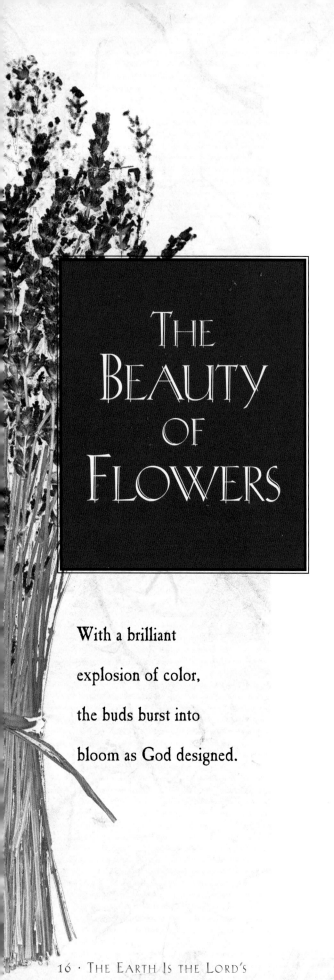

THE BEAUTY OF FLOWERS

With a brilliant

explosion of color,

the buds burst into

bloom as God designed.

I WANDERED LONELY AS A CLOUD

William Wordsworth

I wandered lonely as a cloud
That floats on high o'er vales and hills,
When all at once I saw a crowd,
A host, of golden daffodils;
Beside the lake, beneath the trees,
Fluttering and dancing in the breeze.

Continuous as the stars that shine
And twinkle on the Milky Way,
They stretched in never-ending line
Along the margin of a bay:
Ten thousand saw I at a glance,
Tossing their heads in sprightly dance.

The waves beside them danced; but they
Outdid the sparkling waves in glee;
A poet could not but be gay,
In such a jocund company;
I gazed—and gazed—but little thought
What wealth to me the show had brought:

For oft, when on my couch I lie,
In vacant or in pensive mood,
They flash upon that inward eye
Which is the bliss of solitude;
And then my heart with pleasure fills,
And dances with the daffodils.

THE RHODORA

Ralph Waldo Emerson

In May, when sea-winds pierced our solitudes,
I found the fresh Rhodora in the woods,
Spreading its leafless blooms in a damp nook,
To please the desert and the sluggish brook.
The purple petals, fallen in the pool,
Made the black water with their beauty gay;
Here might the redbird come his plumes to cool,
And court the flower that cheapens his array.

Rhodora! if the sages ask thee why
This charm is wasted on the earth and sky,
Tell them, dear, that if eyes were made for seeing,
Then Beauty is its own excuse for being:
Why thou wert there, O rival of the rose!
I never thought to ask, I never knew:
But, in my simple ignorance, suppose
The selfsame Power that brought me there brought you.

LABURNUM

William Cowper

Laburnum, rich in streaming gold; syringa, ivory pure;
The scentless and the scented rose; this red,
And of an humbler growth, the other tall,
And throwing up into the darkest gloom
Of neighbouring cypress, or more sable yew,
Her silver globes, light as the foamy surf
That the wind severs from the broken wave;
The lilac, various in array, now white,
Now sanguine, and her beauteous head now set
With purple spikes pyramidal, as if,
Studious of ornament, yet unresolved
Which hue she most approved, she chose them all:
Copious of flowers the woodbine, pale and wan,
But well compensating her sickly looks
With never-cloying odours, early and late;
Hypericum all bloom, so thick a swarm
Of flowers, like flies clothing her slender rods,
That scarce a leaf appears; mezereon too,
Though leafless, well attired, and thick beset
With blushing wreaths, investing every spray;
Althæa with the purple eye; the broom,
Yellow and bright as bullion unalloy'd,
Her blossoms; and luxuriant above all
The jasmine, throwing wide her elegant sweets,
The deep dark green of whose unvarnish'd leaf
Makes more conspicuous, and illumines more
The bright profusion of her scatter'd stars.

The heavens declare the glory of God;

and the firmament sheweth his handywork.

Day unto day uttereth speech,

and night unto night sheweth knowledge.

There is no speech nor language,

where their voice is not heard.

Their line is gone out through all the earth,

and their words to the end of the world.

In them hath he set a tabernacle for the sun,

Which is as a bridegroom coming out of his chamber,

and rejoiceth as a strong man to run a race.

His going forth is from the end of the heaven,

and his circuit unto the ends of it:

and there is nothing hid from the heat thereof.

PSALM 19:1-6

Brilliant colors tint the
sunset over Newfound
Lake in New Hampshire.

The Lord by wisdom hath founded the earth;

by understanding hath he established the heavens.

By his knowledge the depths are broken up, and the clouds drop down the dew.

The LORD possessed me in the beginning of his way, before his works of old.

I was set up from everlasting, from the beginning, or ever the earth was.

When there were no depths, I was brought forth; when there were no fountains

abounding with water. Before the mountains were settled, before the hills

was I brought forth: While as yet he had not made the earth, nor the fields,

nor the highest part of the dust of the world. When he prepared the heavens,

I was there: when he set a compass upon the face of the depth:

When he established the clouds above: when he strengthened the fountains

of the deep: When he gave to the sea his decree, that the waters should not

pass his commandment: when he appointed the foundations of the earth:

Then I was by him, as one brought up with him: and I was daily his delight,

rejoicing always before him; Rejoicing in the habitable part of his earth;

and my delights were with the sons of men.

PROVERBS 3:19-20; 8:22-31

A field of daisies is bright with color as
the fog lifts over the Androscoggin
River in New Hampshire.

O give thanks unto the Lord;

for he is good: for his mercy endureth for ever.

O give thanks unto the God of gods: for his mercy endureth for ever.

O give thanks to the LORD of lords: for his mercy endureth for ever.

To him who alone doeth great wonders: for his mercy endureth for ever.

To him that by wisdom made the heavens: for his mercy endureth for ever.

To him that stretched out the earth above the waters:

for his mercy endureth for ever.

To him that made great lights: for his mercy endureth for ever:

The sun to rule by day: for his mercy endureth for ever:

The moon and stars to rule by night: for his mercy endureth for ever.

PSALM 136:1-9

The light from the heavens illuminates the
woods in Alabama's Cheaha State Park.

Consider the lilies of the field,

how they grow; they toil not, neither do they spin:

And yet I say unto you, That even Solomon in all his glory

was not arrayed like one of these. Wherefore, if God so clothe the grass

of the field, which to day is, and to morrow is cast into the oven,

shall he not much more clothe you, O ye of little faith?

Therefore take no thought, saying, What shall we eat? or,

What shall we drink? or, Wherewithal shall we be clothed? . . .

for your heavenly Father knoweth that ye have need of all these things.

But seek ye first the kingdom of God, and his righteousness;

and all these things shall be added unto you.

MATTHEW 6:28B-33

Large-flowered trilliums and fringed
phacelia blanket the forest floor in
Great Smoky Mountains National Park.

This Is My Father's World

Maltbie D. Babcock

Franklin L. Sheppard

1. This is my Fa-ther's world, And to my lis-t'ning ears All
2. This is my Fa-ther's world, The birds their car-ols raise, The

na-ture sings, and round me rings The mu-sic of the spheres.
morn-ing light, the lil-y white, De-clare their Mak-er's praise.

This is my Fa-ther's world: I rest me in the thought Of
This is my Fa-ther's world: He shines in all that's fair; In the

rocks and trees, of skies and seas— His hand the won-ders wrought.
rust-ling grass I hear him pass, He speaks to me ev-'ry-where.

This is my Father's world,

O let me ne'er forget

That though the wrong seems oft so strong,

God is the ruler yet.

This is my Father's world:

The battle is not done;

Jesus who died shall be satisfied

And earth and heav'n be one.

For God is the King of all the earth:
sing ye praises with understanding.
PSALM 47:7

THE GIFTS OF NATURE

Sent by God, rainbows and blossoms grace the landscape with color.

THE LILIES OF THE FIELD

Felicia D. Hemans

Flowers! when the Saviour's calm benignant eye
Fell on your gentle beauty; when from you
That heavenly lesson for all hearts He drew,
Eternal, universal as the sky;
Then in the bosom of your purity
A voice He set as in a temple-shrine,
That life's quick travellers ne'er might pass you by
Unwarned of that sweet oracle divine.
And though too oft its low, celestial sound
By the harsh notes of work-day care is drowned,
And the loud steps of vain unlistening haste;
Yet the great ocean hath no tone of power
Mightier to reach the soul, in thought's hushed hour,
Than yours, ye Lilies! chosen thus and graced!

MY HEART LEAPS UP WHEN I BEHOLD

William Wordsworth

My heart leaps up when I behold
A rainbow in the sky:
So was it when my life began;
So is it now I am a man;
So be it when I shall grow old,
Or let me die!
The Child is father of the Man;
And I could wish my days to be
Bound each to each by natural piety.

THE SNOWDROP

Laetitia Elizabeth Landon

Thou beautiful new comer,
With white and maiden brow;
Thou fairy gift from summer,
Why art thou blooming now?
This dim and sheltered alley
Is dark with winter green;
Not such as in a valley
At sweet springtime is seen.

The lime tree's tender yellow,
The aspen's silvery sheen,
With mingling colours mellow
The universal green.
Now solemn yews are bending
'Mid gloomy fires around;
And in long dark wreaths descending,
The ivy sweeps the ground.

No sweet companion pledges
Thy health as dewdrops pass;
No rose is on the hedges,
No violet in the grass.
Thou art watching, and thou only
Above the earth's snow tomb,
Thus lovely, and thus lonely,
I bless thee for thy bloom.

'Tis the love for long years cherished,
Yet lingering, lorn, and lone;
Though its lovelier lights have perished,
And its earlier hopes are flown.
Though a weary world hath bound it,
With many a heavy thrall,
And the cold and changed surround it,
It blossometh o'er all.

SPRING FLOWERS

John Keble

The loveliest flowers the closest cling to earth,
And they first feel the sun; so violets blue,
So the soft star-like primrose drenched in dew,
The happiest of Spring's happy, fragrant birth.
To gentlest touches sweetest tones reply—
Still humbleness with her low breathed voice
Can steal o'er man's proud heart, and win his choice
From earth to heaven, with mightier witchery
Than eloquence or wisdom e'er could own.
Bloom on then in your shade, contented bloom,
Sweet flowers, nor deem yourselves to all unknown—
Heaven knows you, by whose gales and dews ye thrive
They know, who one day for their altered doom
Shall thank you, taught by you to abase themselves and live.

In the beginning God created the heaven and the earth.

And the earth was without form, and void; and darkness was upon the face of the deep.

And the Spirit of God moved upon the face of the waters. And God said, Let there be light:

and there was light. And God saw the light, that it was good. . . . And God said,

Let us make man in our image, after our likeness. . . . So God created man in his own image,

in the image of God created he him; male and female created he them.

And God blessed them, and God said unto them, Be fruitful, and multiply,

and replenish the earth, and subdue it: and have dominion over the fish of the sea,

and over the fowl of the air, and over every living thing that moveth upon the earth.

And God said, Behold, I have given you every herb bearing seed, which is upon the face

of all the earth, and every tree, in the which is the fruit of a tree yielding seed;

to you it shall be for meat. And to every beast of the earth, and to every fowl of the air,

and to every thing that creepeth upon the earth, wherein there is life,

I have given every green herb for meat: and it was so.

And God saw every thing that he had made, and, behold, it was very good.

GENESIS 1:1-4, 26, 27-31

Redwoods in California
stand tall, straight, and strong.

Give ear, O ye heavens, and I will speak;

and hear, O earth, the words of my mouth.

My doctrine shall drop as the rain,

my speech shall distil as the dew,

as the small rain upon the tender herb,

and as the showers upon the grass:

Because I will publish the name of the Lord:

ascribe ye greatness unto our God.

He is the Rock, his work is perfect:

for all his ways are judgment:

a God of truth and without iniquity,

just and right is he.

DEUTERONOMY 32:1-4

Rain from heaven refreshes the red tulips.

I have seen the travail,

which God hath given

to the sons of men to be exercised in it.

He hath made every thing beautiful in his time:

also he hath set the world in their heart,

so that no man can find out the work

that God maketh from the beginning to the end.

I know that there is no good in them,

but for a man to rejoice, and to do good in his life.

And also that every man should eat and drink,

and enjoy the good of all his labour, it is the gift of God.

ECCLESIASTES 3:10-13

Powerful rushing water breaks
the stillness of the woods at
Noccalula Falls in Alabama.

The Glory of the Lord

Chapter 2

In Virginia's Shenandoah National Park,
the water of Dark Hollow Falls spills
over the moss-covered rocks.

Behold, God is great, and we know him not,

neither can the number of his years be searched out.

For he maketh small the drops of water:

they pour down rain according to the vapour thereof:

Which the clouds do drop and distil upon man abundantly.

Also can any understand the spreadings of the clouds,

or the noise of his tabernacle? Behold, he spreadeth his

light upon it, and covereth the bottom of the sea.

For by them judgeth he the people; he giveth meat in abundance.

With clouds he covereth the light; and commandeth it

not to shine by the cloud that cometh betwixt.

The noise thereof sheweth concerning it,

the cattle also concerning the vapour.

JOB 36:26-33

The colors of the sunset touch Simpson's
Reef, off the coast of Oregon.

Praise ye the LORD. Praise ye the name

of the LORD; praise him, O ye servants of the LORD.

Ye that stand in the house of the LORD, in the courts of the house

of our God. Praise the LORD; for the LORD is good:

sing praises unto his name; for it is pleasant.

For I know that the LORD is great, and that our LORD

is above all gods. Whatsoever the LORD pleased,

that did he in heaven, and in earth, in the seas, and all deep places.

He causeth the vapours to ascend from the ends of the earth;

he maketh lightnings for the rain;

he bringeth the wind out of his treasuries.

PSALM 135:1-3, 5-7

High over the Franconia Range, the
moon bathes New Hampshire's
Mount Lafayette in a heavenly glow.

Bless the LORD, O my soul. O LORD my God,

thou art very great; thou art clothed with honour and majesty.

Who coverest thyself with light as with a garment: who stretchest out the heavens

like a curtain: Who layeth the beams of his chambers in the waters:

who maketh the clouds his chariot: who walketh upon the wings of the wind:

Who maketh his angels spirits; his ministers a flaming fire: Who laid the

foundations of the earth, that it should not be removed for ever.

Thou coveredst it with the deep as with a garment: the waters stood above

the mountains. At thy rebuke they fled; at the voice of thy thunder

they hasted away. They go up by the mountains; they go down by the valleys

unto the place which thou hast founded for them. Thou hast set a bound

that they may not pass over; that they turn not again to cover the earth.

PSALM 104:1-9

The waters of Lake Superior are tranquil at the base
of Miners Castle, a sandstone cliff in Michigan.

O Worship the King

Robert Grant

Johann Michael Haydn

1. O worship the King, all-glorious above;
2. O tell of his might, O sing of his grace,

O gratefully sing his power and his love;
Whose robe is the light, Whose canopy space.

Our Shield and Defender, the Ancient of Days,
His chariots of wrath the deep thunderclouds form,

Pavilioned in splendor, and girded with praise.
And dark is his path on the wings of the storm.

Thy bountiful care, what tongue can recite?

It breathes in the air, it shines in the light,

It streams from the hills, it descends to the plain,

And sweetly distills in the dew and the rain.

Frail children of dust, and feeble as frail,

In thee do we trust, nor find thee to fail;

Thy mercies how tender, how firm to the end!

Our Maker, Defender, Redeemer, and Friend.

THE GLORY OF THE SKIES

From the expanse of

clouds above the earth,

God sends the water

that renews and the

light that strengthens.

I LOVE THEE NATURE WITH A BOUNDLESS LOVE

John Clare

I love thee nature with a boundless love,
The calm of earth, the storms of roaring woods
The winds that breathe happiness where e'er I rove.
There's life's own music in the swelling floods
My harp is in the thunder melting clouds,
The snow capped mountain, and the rolling sea
And hear ye not the voice where darkness shrouds
The heavens—there lives happiness for me.

EARTH AND HEAVEN

John Keble

When I behold yon arch magnificent
Spanning the gorgeous West, the autumnal bed
Where the great Sun now hides his weary head,
With here and there a purple isle, that rent
From that huge cloud their solid continent,
Seem floating in a sea of golden light,
A fire is kindled in my musing Sprite,
And Fancy whispers: Such the glories lent
To this our mortal life; most glowing fair,
But built on clouds, and melting while we gaze.
Yet since those shadowy lights sure witness bear
Of One not seen, the Undying Sun and Source
Of good and fair, who wisely them surveys
Will use them well to cheer his heavenward course.

GOD'S GRANDEUR

Gerard Manley Hopkins

The world is charged with the grandeur of God.
It will flame out, like shining from shook foil;
It gathers to a greatness, like the ooze of oil
Crushed. Why do men then now not reck his rod?
Generations have trod, have trod, have trod;
And all is seared with trade; bleared, smeared with toil;
And wears man's smudge and shares man's smell: the soil
Is bare now, nor can foot feel, being shod.
And for all this, nature is never spent;
There lives the dearest freshness deep down things;
And though the last lights off the black West went
Oh, morning, at the brown brink eastward, springs—
Because the Holy Ghost over the bent
World broods with warm breast and with ah! bright wings.

THE CLOUD

Percy Bysshe Shelley

I bring fresh showers for the thirsting flowers,
From the seas and the streams;
I bear light shade for the leaves when laid
In their noonday dreams.
From my wings are shaken the dews that waken
The sweet buds every one,
When rocked to rest on their mother's breast,
As she dances about the sun.
I wield the flail of the lashing hail,
And whiten the green plains under,
And then again I dissolve it in rain,
And laugh as I pass in thunder.

I am the daughter of earth and water,
And the nursling of the sky;
I pass through the pores of the ocean and shores;
I change, but I cannot die.
For after the rain when with never a stain
The pavilion of Heaven is bare,
And the winds and sunbeams with their convex gleams
Build up the blue dome of air,
I silently laugh at my own cenotaph,
And out of the caverns of rain,
Like a child from the womb, like a ghost from the tomb,
I arise and unbuild it again.

O LORD, how manifold are thy works!

in wisdom hast thou made them all: the earth is full

of thy riches. So is this great and wide sea, wherein

are things creeping innumerable, both small and great beasts.

The glory of the LORD shall endure for ever:

the LORD shall rejoice in his works. He looketh on the earth,

and it trembleth: he toucheth the hills, and they smoke.

I will sing unto the LORD as long as I live:

I will sing praise to my God while I have my being.

My meditation of him shall be sweet:

I will be glad in the LORD.

PSALM 104:24-25, 31-34

Lush, green tulip poplars fill the valley
below Tennessee's Mount Le Conte
in the Great Smoky Mountains.

nd the same day, when the even was come,

he saith unto them, Let us pass over unto the other side.

And when they had sent away the multitude, they took him

even as he was in the ship. And there were also with him other little ships.

And there arose a great storm of wind, and the waves beat into the ship,

so that it was now full. And he was in the hinder part of the ship,

asleep on a pillow: and they awake him, and say unto him,

Master, carest thou not that we perish? And he arose, and rebuked the

wind, and said unto the sea, Peace, be still. And the wind ceased,

and there was a great calm. And he said unto them, Why are ye so fearful?

how is it that ye have no faith? And they feared exceedingly,

and said one to another, What manner of man is this,

that even the wind and the sea obey him?

MARK 4:35-41

A rainbow breaks through the clouds over a
calm Newfound Lake in New Hampshire.

O come, let us sing unto the LORD:

let us make a joyful noise to the rock of our salvation.

Let us come before his presence with thanksgiving,

and make a joyful noise unto him with psalms.

For the LORD is a great God, and a great King above all

gods. In his hand are the deep places of the earth:

the strength of the hills is his also. The sea is his,

and he made it: and his hands formed the dry land.

O come, let us worship and bow down:

let us kneel before the LORD our maker. For he is our God,

and we are the people of his pasture,

and the sheep of his hand.

PSALM 95:1-7

Clouds rest in the treetops of
Yellowstone's Dunraven Pass.

W here wast thou when I laid the foundations of the earth?

declare, if thou hast understanding. Who hath laid the measures thereof, if thou knowest?

or who hath stretched the line upon it? Whereupon are the foundations thereof fastened?

or who laid the corner stone thereof; When the morning stars sang together,

and all the sons of God shouted for joy? Or who shut up the sea with doors,

when it brake forth, as if it had issued out of the womb? When I made the cloud

the garment thereof, and thick darkness a swaddlingband for it, And brake up for it

my decreed place, and set bars and doors, And said, Hitherto shalt thou come,

but no further: and here shall thy proud waves be stayed?

Hast thou perceived the breadth of the earth? declare if thou knowest it all.

Where is the way where light dwelleth? and as for darkness, where is the place thereof,

That thou shouldest take it to the bound thereof, and that thou shouldest know the paths

to the house thereof? Knowest thou it, because thou wast then born?

or because the number of thy days is great?

JOB 38:4-11, 18-21

Clouds float above the rocks
at Oregon's Ecola State Park.

I will extol thee, my God, O king;

and I will bless thy name for ever and ever.

Every day will I bless thee; and I will praise thy name for ever and ever.

Great is the LORD, and greatly to be praised; and his greatness

is unsearchable. One generation shall praise thy works to another,

and shall declare thy mighty acts. I will speak of the glorious honour

of thy majesty, and of thy wondrous works. And men shall speak

of the might of thy terrible acts: and I will declare thy greatness.

They shall abundantly utter the memory of thy great goodness,

and shall sing of thy righteousness. The LORD is gracious,

and full of compassion; slow to anger, and of great mercy.

The LORD is good to all: and his tender mercies are over all his works.

PSALM 145:1-9

Across from Lubec, Maine, an expanse of
rosebushes blooms alongside the water.

P raise ye the Lord: for it is good to sing

praises unto our God; for it is pleasant; and praise is comely. He telleth the

number of the stars; he calleth them all by their names. Great is our Lord,

and of great power: his understanding is infinite. He sendeth forth

his commandment upon earth: his word runneth very swiftly.

He giveth snow like wool: he scattereth the hoarfrost like ashes.

He casteth forth his ice like morsels: who can stand before his cold?

He sendeth out his word, and melteth them: he causeth his wind to blow,

and the waters flow. He hath made the earth by his power, he hath

established the world by his wisdom, and hath stretched out the heaven

by his understanding. When he uttereth his voice, there is a multitude

of waters in the heavens; and he causeth the vapours to ascend

from the ends of the earth: he maketh lightnings with rain,

and bringeth forth the wind out of his treasures.

PSALM 147:1, 4-5, 15-18; JEREMIAH 51:15-16

Water vapors float across the rock
ledge at Pemaquid Point in Maine.

With Glory Clad, with Strength Arrayed

Nahum Tate and Nicholas Brady

German

1. With glo - ry clad, with strength ar - rayed,
2. How sure - ly stab - lished is thy throne,

The Lord, that o'er all na - ture reigns,
Which shall no change or per - iod see!

The world's foun - da - tions strong - ly laid,
For thou, O Lord, and thou a - lone,

And the vast fab - ric still sus - tains.
Art God from all e - ter - ni - ty.

The floods, O Lord, lift up their voice,

And toss the troubled waves on high;

But God above can still their noise,

And make the angry sea comply.

Thy promise, Lord, is ever sure,

And they that in thy house would dwell,

That happy station to secure,

Must still in holiness excel.

THE PEACE OF CREATION

The heavens and earth change daily, yet their presence is unmoved.

PIED BEAUTY

Gerard Manley Hopkins

Glory be to God for dappled things—
For skies of couple-color as a brindled cow;
For rose-moles all in stipple upon trout that swim;
Fresh-firecoal chestnut-falls; finches' wings;
Landscape plotted and pieced—fold, fallow, and plow;
And all trades, their gear and tackle and trim.

All things counter, original, spare, strange;
Whatever is fickle, freckled (who knows how?)
With swift, slow; sweet, sour; adazzle, dim;
He fathers-forth whose beauty is past change:
Praise Him.

THE EVENING CLOUD

John Wilson

A cloud lay cradled near the setting sun,
A gleam of crimson tinged its braided snow;
Long had I watched the glory moving on,
O'er the still radiance of the Lake below;
Tranquil its spirit seemed and floated slow;
Even in its very motion there was rest;
While every breath of eve that chanced to blow,
Wafted the traveller to the beauteous West.
Emblem, methought, of the departed soul,
To whose white robe the gleam of bliss is given;
And by the breath of mercy made to roll
Right onwards to the golden gates of Heaven;
Where to the eye of Faith it peaceful lies,
And tells to man his glorious destinies.

HOW STILL, HOW HAPPY

Emily Brontë

How still, how happy! Those are words
That once would scarce agree together;
I loved the plashing of the surge,
The changing heaven, the breezy weather,

More than smooth seas and cloudless skies
And solemn, soothing, softened airs
That in the solemn forest woke no sighs
And from the green spray shook no tears.

How still, how happy! Now I feel
Where silence dwells is sweeter far
Than laughing mirth's most rapturous swell
However pure its raptures are.

Come, sit down on this sunny stone:
'Tis wintry light o'er flowerless moors—
But sit—for we are all alone
And clear expands heaven's breathless shores.

I could think in the withered grass
Spring's budding wreaths we might discern;
The violet's eye might shyly flash
And young leaves shoot among the fern.

It is but thought—full many a night
The snow shall clothe those hills afar
And storms shall add a drearier blight
And winds shall wage a wilder war,

Before the lark may herald in
Fresh foliage twined with blossoms fair
And summer days again begin
Their glory-haloed crown to wear.

Yet my heart loves December's smile
As much as July's golden beam;
Then let us sit and watch the while
The blue ice curdling on the stream.

GOD'S WORLD

Edna St. Vincent Millay

O world, I cannot hold thee close enough!
Thy winds, thy wide grey skies!
Thy mists, that roll and rise!
Thy woods, this autumn day, that ache and sag
And all but cry with colour! That gaunt crag
To crush! To lift the lean of that black bluff!
World, World, I cannot get thee close enough!

Long have I known a glory in it all,
But never knew I this;
Here such a passion is
As stretcheth me apart—Lord, I do fear
Thou'st made the world too beautiful this year;
My soul is all but out of me—let fall
No burning leaf; prithee, let no bird call.

W ho hath measured the waters in the hollow of his hand,

and meted out heaven with the span, and comprehended the dust of the earth

in a measure, and weighed the mountains in scales, and the hills in a balance?

Lift up your eyes on high, and behold who hath created these things,

that bringeth out their host by number: he calleth them all by names

by the greatness of his might, for that he is strong in power; not one faileth.

Hast thou not known? hast thou not heard, that the everlasting God, the LORD,

the Creator of the ends of the earth, fainteth not, neither is weary?

there is no searching of his understanding. He giveth power to the faint;

and to them that have no might he increaseth strength. Even the youths shall faint

and be weary, and the young men shall utterly fall: But they that wait upon the

LORD shall renew their strength; they shall mount up with wings as eagles;

they shall run, and not be weary; and they shall walk, and not faint.

ISAIAH 40:12, 26, 28-31

The waters of Taughannock Falls, in New
York, spill out from between the rocks.

The wilderness and the solitary place shall be glad for them;

and the desert shall rejoice, and blossom as the rose. It shall blossom abundantly,

and rejoice even with joy and singing: the glory of Lebanon shall be given unto it,

the excellency of Carmel and Sharon, they shall see the glory of the LORD, and the

excellency of our God. Strengthen ye the weak hands, and confirm the feeble knees.

Say to them that are of a fearful heart, Be strong, fear not: behold, your God

will come with vengeance, even God with a recompence; he will come and save you.

Then the eyes of the blind shall be opened, and the ears of the deaf shall be

unstopped. Then shall the lame man leap as an hart, and the tongue of the dumb sing:

for in the wilderness shall waters break out, and streams in the desert.

And the parched ground shall become a pool, and the thirsty land springs of water:

in the habitation of dragons, where each lay, shall be grass with reeds and rushes.

And the ransomed of the LORD shall return, and come to Zion with songs and

everlasting joy upon their heads: they shall obtain joy and gladness,

and sorrow and sighing shall flee away.

ISAIAH 35:1-7, 10

The paintbrush flowers blossom abundantly amidst the
Navajo sandstone at Arches National Park in Utah.

Ogive thanks unto the LORD,

for he is good: for his mercy endureth for ever.

They that go down to the sea in ships, that do business in great waters;

These see the works of the LORD, and his wonders in the deep.

For he commandeth, and raiseth the stormy wind, which lifteth up

the waves thereof. They mount up to the heaven, they go down again

to the depths: their soul is melted because of trouble. They reel

to and fro, and stagger like a drunken man, and are at their wit's end.

Then they cry unto the LORD in their trouble, and he bringeth them out

of their distresses. He maketh the storm a calm, so that the waves

thereof are still. Then are they glad because they be quiet; so he bringeth

them unto their desired haven. Oh that men would praise the LORD

for his goodness, and for his wonderful works to the children of men!

PSALM 107:1, 23-31

The sun rises over Anemone Cave
at Frenchman Bay in Maine.

ALL CREATURES GREAT AND SMALL

CHAPTER 3

T he LORD is my shepherd; I shall not want.

He maketh me to lie down in green pastures:

he leadeth me beside the still waters.

He restoreth my soul: he leadeth me in the paths

of righteousness for his name's sake.

Yea, though I walk through the valley of the shadow of death,

I will fear no evil: for thou art with me;

thy rod and thy staff they comfort me.

Thou preparest a table before me in the

presence of mine enemies: thou anointest my head with oil;

my cup runneth over. Surely goodness and mercy

shall follow me all the days of my life:

and I will dwell in the house of the LORD for ever.

PSALM 23

At Rhode Island's Coggeshall Farm
Museum, sheep graze the green pastures.

And God said, Let the waters bring forth

abundantly the moving creature that hath life, and fowl

that may fly above the earth in the open firmament of heaven.

And God created great whales, and every living creature that moveth,

which the waters brought forth abundantly, after their kind,

and every winged fowl after his kind: and God saw that it was good.

And God blessed them, saying, Be fruitful, and multiply,

and fill the waters in the seas, and let fowl multiply in the earth.

And God said, Let the earth bring forth the living creature after his kind, cattle,

and creeping thing, and beast of the earth after his kind:

and it was so. And God made the beast of the earth after his kind,

and cattle after their kind, and every thing that creepeth upon the earth

after his kind: and God saw that it was good.

GENESIS 1:20-22, 24-25

Graceful swans float along the clear blue water.

O LORD, our LORD, how excellent is thy name

in all the earth! who hast set thy glory above the heavens.

Out of the mouth of babes and sucklings hast thou ordained strength

because of thine enemies, that thou mightest still the enemy

and the avenger. When I consider thy heavens, the work of thy fingers,

the moon and the stars, which thou hast ordained; What is man,

that thou art mindful of him? and the son of man,

that thou visitest him? For thou hast made him a little lower

than the angels, and hast crowned him with glory and honour.

Thou madest him to have dominion over the works of thy hands;

thou hast put all things under his feet: All sheep and oxen, yea,

and the beasts of the field; The fowl of the air, and the fish of the sea,

and whatsoever passeth through the paths of the seas.

O LORD our Lord, how excellent is thy name in all the earth!

PSALM 8

A young lynx sits, alert, in the snowy woods.

ALL THINGS BRIGHT AND BEAUTIFUL

Cecil Frances Alexander

Dick Torrans

1. The lit - tle flow'r that o - pens, The lit - tle bird that sings,
2. The cold wind in the win - ter, The pleas - ant sum - mer sun,

God made their glow - ing col - ors, He made their ti - ny wings.
The ripe fruits in the gar - den, He made them ev - 'ry one.

All things bright and beau - ti - ful, All crea - tures great and small,

All things wise and won - der - ful, The Lord God made them all.

He gave us eyes to see them,

And lips that we might tell

How great is God Almighty,

Who has made all things well.

All things bright and beautiful,

Creatures great and small,

All things wise and wonderful,

The Lord God made them all.

Let every thing that hath breath
praise the LORD.
Praise ye the Lord.
PSALM 150:6

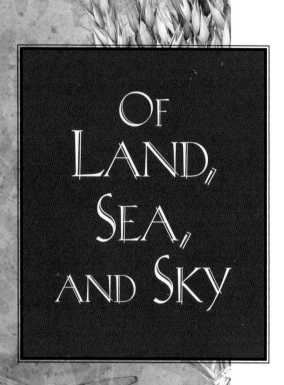

Of Land, Sea, and Sky

From the birds that glide through the air to the beasts that gallop across the land, animals are a divine creation.

To a Skylark

William Wordsworth

Ethereal minstrel! pilgrim of the sky!
Dost thou despise the earth where cares abound?
Or, while the wings aspire, are heart and eye
Both with thy nest upon the dewy ground?
Thy nest which thou canst drop into at will,
Those quivering wings composed, that music still!

Leave to the nightingale her shady wood;
A privacy of glorious light is thine;
Whence thou dost pour upon the world a flood
Of harmony, with instinct more divine;
Type of the wise who soar, but never roam;
True to the kindred points of Heaven and Home!

The Lamb

William Blake

Little Lamb, who made thee?
Dost thou know who made thee?
Gave thee life, and bid thee feed
By the stream and o'er the mead;
Gave thee clothing of delight,
Softest clothing, woolly, bright;
Gave thee such a tender voice,
Making all the vales rejoice?
Little Lamb, who made thee?
Dost thou know who made thee?

Little Lamb, I'll tell thee,
Little Lamb, I'll tell thee:
He is callèd by thy name,
For he calls himself a Lamb.
He is meek, and he is mild;
He became a little child.
I a child, and thou a lamb,
We are callèd by his name.
Little Lamb, God bless thee!
Little Lamb, God bless thee!

THE WILD SWANS AT COOLE

W. B. Yeats

The trees are in their autumn beauty,
The woodland paths are dry;
Under the October twilight the water
Mirrors a still sky.
Upon the brimming water among the stones
Are nine and fifty swans.

The nineteenth autumn has come upon me
Since I first made my count.
I saw, before I had well finished,
All suddenly mount
And scatter wheeling in great broken rings
Upon their clamorous wings.

But now they drift on the still water
Mysterious, beautiful.
Among what rushes will they build,
By what lake's edge or pool
Delight men's eyes when I awake some day
To find they have flown away?

THE EAGLE

Alfred, Lord Tennyson

He clasps the crag with crooked hands;
Close to the sun in lonely lands,
Ringed with the azure world, he stands.
The wrinkled sea beneath him crawls;
He watches from his mountain walls,
And like a thunderbolt he falls.

THE TYGER

William Blake

Tyger! tyger! burning bright
In the forests of the night,
What immortal hand or eye
Could frame thy fearful symmetry?

In what distant deeps or skies
Burnt the fire of thine eyes?
On what wings dare he aspire?
What the hand dare seize the fire?

And what shoulder, and what art,
Could twist the sinews of thy heart?
And when thy heart began to beat,
What dread hand? and what dread feet?

What the hammer? what the chain?
In what furnace was thy brain?
What the anvil? What dread grasp
Dare its deadly terrors clasp?

When the stars threw down their spears,
And watered heaven with their tears,
Did he smile his work to see?
Did he who made the lamb make thee?

Tyger! tyger! burning bright
In the forests of the night,
What immortal hand or eye,
Dare frame thy fearful symmetry?

Wilt thou hunt the prey for the lion?

or fill the appetite of the young lions. When they couch in their dens, and abide

in the covert to lie in wait? Who provideth for the raven his food?

Who hath sent out the wild ass free? or who hath loosed the bands of the wild ass?

Whose house I have made the wilderness, and the barren land his dwellings.

He scorneth the multitude of the city, neither regardeth he the crying of the driver.

The range of the mountains is his pasture, and he searcheth after every green thing.

Gavest thou the goodly wings unto the peacocks? or wings and feathers unto the

ostrich? Hast thou given the horse strength? hast thou clothed his neck with thunder?

Canst thou make him afraid as a grasshopper? the glory of his nostrils is terrible.

He paweth in the valley, and rejoiceth in his strength: he goeth on to meet the armed men.

Doth the hawk fly by thy wisdom, and stretch her wings toward the south?

Doth the eagle mount up at thy command, and make her nest on high?

She dwelleth and abideth on the rock, upon the crag of the rock, and the strong place.

From thence she seeketh the prey, and her eyes behold afar off.

JOB 38:39-41; 39:5-8, 13, 19-21, 26-29

A horse rests peacefully in the pasture
among the bluebonnets in Texas.

Go to the ant, thou sluggard;

consider her ways, and be wise: Which having no guide,

overseer, or ruler, Provideth her meat in the summer,

and gathereth her food in the harvest.

There be four things which are little upon the earth,

but they are exceeding wise: The ants are a people

not strong, yet they prepare their meat in the summer;

The conies are but a feeble folk, yet make they their

houses in the rocks; The locusts have no king,

yet go they forth all of them by bands; The spider

taketh hold with her hands, and is in kings' palaces.

PROVERBS 6:6-8, 30:24-28

Maple saplings give shade
and sustenance to the creatures
that share the woods.

ALL CREATURES OF OUR GOD AND KING

Francis of Assisi

German Melody

1. All crea-tures of our God and King, lift up your voice and with us sing
2. Thou rush-ing wind that art so strong, you clouds that sail in heav'n a-long,

Al-le-lu-ia, Al-le-lu-ia! Thou burn-ing sun with gold-en beam,
O praise him, Al-le-lu-ia! Thou ris-ing morn in praise re-joice,

Thou sil-ver moon with soft-er gleam, O praise him, O praise him,
You lights of eve-ning, find a voice, O praise him, O praise him,

Al-le-lu-ia, al-le-lu-ia, al-le-lu-ia.

Thou flowing water, pure and clear,
Make music for thy Lord to hear,
Alleluia, Alleluia!
Thou fire so masterful and bright,
That givest man both warmth and light,
O praise him, O praise him,
Alleluia, alleluia, alleluia.

And all you men of tender heart,
Forgiving others, take your part,
O sing ye, Alleluia!
You who long pain and sorrow bear,
Praise God and on him cast your care,
O praise him, O praise him,
Alleluia, alleluia, alleluia.

Let all things their Creator bless,
And worship him in humbleness,
O praise him, Alleluia!
Praise, praise the Father, praise the Son,
And praise the Spirit, Three in One,
O praise him, O praise him,
Alleluia, alleluia, alleluia.

OF FLOWER, FIELD, AND TREE

The creatures of the earth share the home that the Lord provides.

TO A WATER BIRD

Lord Edward Thurlow

O melancholy bird—a winter's day
Thou standest by the margin of the pool,
And taught by God dost the whole being school
To patience, which all evil can allay;
God has appointed thee the fish thy prey;
And given thyself a lesson to the fool
Unthrifty, to submit to moral rule,
And his unthinking course by thee to weigh.
There need not schools, nor the professor's chair,
Though these be good, true widsom to impart;
He who has not enough for these to spare
Of time or gold, may yet amend his heart,
And teach his soul by brooks and rivers fair;
Nature is always wise in every part.

TO THE GRASSHOPPER AND THE CRICKET

James Henry Leigh Hunt

Green little vaulter in the sunny grass,
Catching your heart up at the feel of June,
Sole voice that's heard amidst the lazy noon,
When even the bees lag at the summoning brass,
And you, warm little housekeeper, who class
With those who think the candles come too soon,
Loving the fire, and with your tricksome tune
Nick the glad silent moments as they pass;
Oh sweet and tiny cousins, that belong,
One to the fields, the other to the hearth,
Both have your sunshine; both, though small, are strong
At your clear hearts; and both seem given to earth
To ring in thoughtful ears this natural song—
In doors and out, summer and winter, mirth.

To a Butterfly

William Wordsworth

I've watched you now a full half-hour,
Self-poised upon that yellow flower;
And, little Butterfly! indeed
I know not if you sleep or feed.
How motionless! not frozen seas
More motionless! and then
What joy awaits you, when the breeze
Hath found you out among the trees,
And calls you forth again!

This plot of orchard-ground is ours;
My trees they are, my sister's flowers;
Here rest your wings when they are weary;
Here lodge as in a sanctuary!
Come often to us, fear no wrong;
Sit near us on the bough!
We'll talk of sunshine and of song,
And summer days, when we were young;
Sweet childish days, that were as long
As twenty days are now.

The Thrush's Nest

John Clare

Within a thick and spreading hawthorn bush,
That overhung a molehill large and round,
I heard from morn to morn a merry thrush
Sing hymns of rapture, while I drank the sound
With joy—and oft, an unintruding guest,
I watched her secret toils from day to day;
How true she warped the moss to form her nest,
And modelled it with wood and clay.
And by and by, like heath-bells gilt with dew,
There lay her shining eggs as bright as flowers,
Ink-spotted over, shells of green and blue:
And there I witnessed in the summer hours
A brood of nature's minstrels chirp and fly,
Glad as the sunshine and the laughing sky.

I Think I Know No Finer Things Than Dogs

Hally Carrington Brent

Though prejudices perhaps my mind befogs,
I think I know no finer things than dogs:
The young ones, they of gay and bounding heart,
Who lure us in their games to take a part,
Who with mock tragedy their antics cloak
And, from their wild eyes' tail, admit the joke;
The old ones, with their wistful, fading eyes,
They who desire no further paradise
Than the warm comfort of our smile and hand,
Who tune their moods to ours and understand
Each word and gesture; they who lie and wait
To welcome us—with no rebuke if late.
Sublime the love they bear; but ask to live
Close to our feet, unrecompensed to give;
Beside which many men seem very logs—
I think I know no finer things than dogs.

And God spake unto Noah, saying, Go forth of the ark,

thou, and thy wife, and thy sons, and thy sons' wives with thee.

Bring forth with thee every living thing that is with thee, of all flesh,

both of fowl, and of cattle, and of every creeping thing that creepeth upon the earth;

that they may breed abundantly in the earth, and be fruitful, and multiply

upon the earth. And Noah went forth, and his sons, and his wife,

and his sons' wives with him: Every beast, every creeping thing, and every fowl,

and whatsoever creepeth upon the earth, after their kinds, went forth out of the ark.

And God spake unto Noah, and to his sons with him, saying, And I, behold,

I establish my covenant with you, and with your seed after you; And with

every living creature that is with you, of the fowl, of the cattle, and of every beast

of the earth with you; from all that go out of the ark, to every beast of the earth.

And I will establish my covenant with you, neither shall all flesh be cut off any more

by the waters of a flood; neither shall there any more be a flood to destroy the earth.

GENESIS 8:15-19; 9:8-11

Blessed by the cover of snow and the thickness
of fur, the Arctic foxes are safe and warm.

He sendeth the springs into the valleys,

which run among the hills. They give drink to every beast of the field:

the wild asses quench their thirst. By them shall the fowls of the heaven

have their habitation, which sing among the branches.

He watereth the hills from his chambers: the earth is satisfied

with the fruit of thy works. The trees of the LORD are full of sap;

the cedars of Lebanon, which he hath planted; Where the birds

make their nests: as for the stork, the fir trees are her house.

The high hills are a refuge for the wild goats; and the rocks

for the conies. He appointed the moon for seasons: the sun knoweth

his going down. Thou makest darkness, and it is night: wherein all the

beasts of the forest do creep forth. The young lions roar after their prey,

and seek their meat from God. The sun ariseth, they gather themselves

together, and lay them down in their dens. Man goeth forth unto his work

and to his labour until the evening.

PSALM 104:10-13, 16-23

The renewing water of Smith Creek flows
through Washington's Olympic National Park.

$\mathbb{B}$ut ask now the beasts,

and they shall teach thee;

and the fowls of the air, and they shall tell thee:

Or speak to the earth, and it shall teach thee:

and the fishes of the sea shall declare unto thee.

Who knoweth not in all these that the hand of the LORD

hath wrought this? In whose hand is the soul

of every living thing, and the breath of all mankind.

JOB 12:7-10

Draft horses build their strength
from the grasses grown on the land.

The Fruit of the Land

Chapter 4

The sun rises over an apple orchard
in Virginia, where dandelions bloom
amidst the fruit trees.

And God said, Let the earth bring forth grass,

the herb yielding seed, and the fruit tree yielding fruit after his kind,

whose seed is in itself, upon the earth: and it was so.

And the earth brought forth grass, and herb yielding seed after his kind,

and the tree yielding fruit, whose seed was in itself,

after his kind: and God saw that it was good.

GENESIS 1:11-12

Under a clear blue sky, the golden
wheat fields sway in the sun.

He causeth the grass to grow for the cattle,

and herb for the service of man: that he may bring forth food

out of the earth; And wine that maketh glad the heart of man,

and oil to make his face to shine,

and bread which strengtheneth man's heart.

O LORD, how manifold are thy works!

in wisdom hast thou made them all: the earth is full of thy riches.

That thou givest them they gather: thou openest thine hand,

they are filled with good. Thou hidest thy face,

they are troubled: thou takest away their breath, they die,

and return to their dust. Thou sendest forth thy spirit,

they are created: and thou renewest the face of the earth.

PSALM 104:14-15, 24, 28-30

Cattle graze on the fruit of the
land in the shadow of Mount
Monadnock in New Hampshire.

Blessed is the man that trusteth in the LORD,

and whose hope the LORD is. For he shall be as a tree planted

by the waters, and that spreadeth out her roots by the river,

and shall not see when heat cometh, but her leaf shall be green;

and shall not be careful in the year of drought,

neither shall cease from yielding fruit.

Blessed is the man that walketh not in the counsel of the ungodly,

nor standeth in the way of sinners, nor sitteth in the seat

of the scornful. But his delight is in the law of the LORD;

and in his law doth he meditate day and night. And he shall be

like a tree planted by the rivers of water, that bringeth forth his fruit

in his season; his leaf also shall not wither;

and whatsoever he doeth shall prosper.

JEREMIAH 17:7-8; PSALM 1:1-3

In the springtime, the apple tree blossoms.

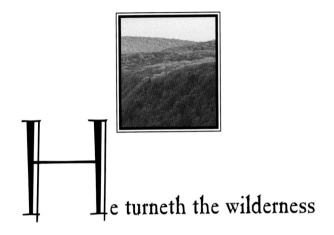

He turneth the wilderness

into a standing water, and dry ground into watersprings.

And there he maketh the hungry to dwell,

that they may prepare a city for habitation;

And sow the fields, and plant vineyards,

which may yield fruits of increase. He blesseth them also,

so that they are multiplied greatly;

and suffereth not their cattle to decrease.

PSALM 107:35-38

The verdant trees fill the landscape at
Pine Creek Gorge in Pennsylvania.

Then judgment shall dwell in the wilderness,

and righteousness remain in the fruitful field.

And the work of righteousness shall be peace;

and the effect of righteousness quietness and assurance for ever.

And my people shall dwell in a peaceable habitation,

and in sure dwellings, and in quiet resting places;

When it shall hail, coming down on the forest;

and the city shall be low in a low place.

Blessed are ye that sow beside all waters,

that send forth thither the feet of the ox and the ass.

The LORD is exalted; for he dwelleth on high:

he hath filled Zion with judgment and righteousness.

And wisdom and knowledge shall be the stability of thy times,

and strength of salvation: the fear of the LORD is his treasure.

ISAIAH 32:16-20, 33:5-6

Brilliant colors adorn the plants and flowers.

B e thou diligent to know the state

of thy flocks, and look well to thy herds.

For riches are not for ever:

and doth the crown endure to every generation?

The hay appeareth, and the tender grass sheweth itself,

and herbs of the mountains are gathered. The lambs

are for thy clothing, and the goats are the price of the field.

And thou shalt have goats' milk enough for thy food,

for the food of thy household,

and for the maintenance for thy maidens.

PROVERBS 27:23-27

The red pines and sugar
maples flourish in these
New Hampshire woods.

We Plow the Fields

Matthias Claudius

Johann A. P. Schulz

1. We plow the fields and scat - ter the good seed on the
2. He on - ly is the Mak - er of all things near and

land, But it is fed and wa - tered by
far; He paints the way - side flow - er, he

God's al - might - y hand; He sends the snow in
lights the eve - ning star; The winds and waves o -

win - ter, the warmth to swell the grain, The
bey him, by him the birds are fed; Much

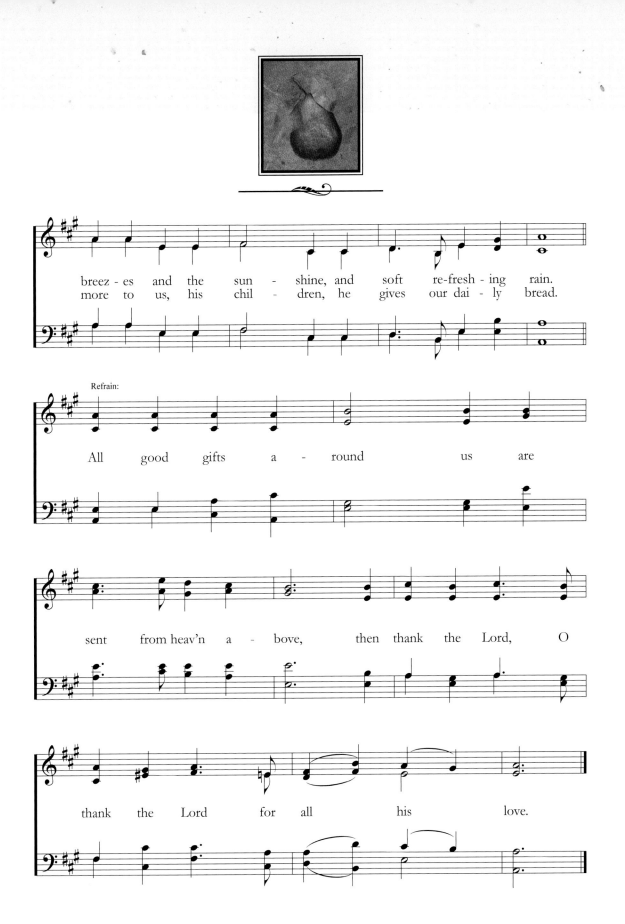

breez - es and the sun - shine, and soft re-fresh - ing rain.
more to us, his chil - dren, he gives our dai - ly bread.

Refrain:

All good gifts a - round us are

sent from heav'n a - bove, then thank the Lord, O

thank the Lord for all his love.

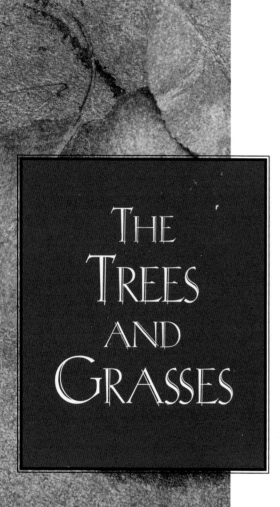

THE TREES AND GRASSES

The land is clothed in
the colors of the plants,
painted by God in hues
of green and gold.

THE HEART OF THE TREE

Henry Cuyler Bunner

What does he plant who plants a tree?
He plants a friend of sun and sky;
He plants the flag of breezes free;
The shaft of beauty, towering high;
He plants a home to heaven anigh
For song and mother-croon of bird
In hushed and happy twilight heard—
The treble of heaven's harmony—
These things he plants who plants a tree.

What does he plant who plants a tree?
He plants cool shade and tender rain,
And seed and bud of days to be,
And years that fade and flush again;
He plants the glory of the plain;
He plants the forest's heritage;
The harvest of a coming age;
The joy that unborn eyes shall see—
These things he plants who plants a tree.

What does he plant who plants a tree?
He plants, in sap and leaf and wood,
In love of home and loyalty
And far-cast thought of civic good—
His blessings on the neighborhood
Who in the hollow of His hand
Holds all the growth of all our land—
A nation's growth from sea to sea
Stirs in his heart who plants a tree.

Song of the Chattahoochee

Sidney Lanier

Out of the hills of Habersham,
Down the valleys of Hall,
I hurry amain to reach the plain,
Run the rapid and leap the fall,
Split at the rock and together again,
Accept my bed, or narrow or wide,
And flee from folly on every side
With a lover's pain to attain the plain
Far from the hills of Habersham,
Far from the valleys of Hall.

All down the hills of Habersham,
All through the valleys of Hall,
The rushes cried Abide, abide,
The willful waterweeds held me thrall,
The laving laurel turned my tide,
The ferns and the fondling grass said Stay,
The dewberry dipped for to work delay,
And the little reeds sighed Abide, abide,
Here in the hills of Habersham,
Here in the valleys of Hall.

High o'er the hills of Habersham,
Veiling the valleys of Hall,
The hickory told me manifold
Fair tales of shade, the poplar tall
Wrought me her shadowy self to hold,

The chestnut, the oak, the walnut, the pine,
Overleaning with flickering meaning and sign,
Said, Pass not, so cold, these manifold
Deep shades of the hills of Habersham,
These glades in the valleys of Hall.

And oft in the hills of Habersham,
And oft in the valleys of Hall,
The white quartz shone, and the smooth brook-stone
Did bar me of passage with friendly brawl,
And many a luminous jewel lone—
Crystals clear or a-cloud with mist,
Ruby, garnet, and amethyst—
Made lures with the lights of streaming stone
In the clefts of the hills of Habersham,
In the beds of the valleys of Hall.

But oh, not the hills of Habersham,
And oh, not the valleys of Hall
Avail: I am fain for to water the plain.
Downward the voices of Duty call—
Downward, to toil and be mixed with the main;
The dry fields burn, and the mills are to turn,
And a myriad flowers mortally yearn,
And the lordly main from beyond the plain
Calls o'er the hills of Habersham,
Calls through the valleys of Hall.

In that day sing ye unto her,

A vineyard of red wine. I the LORD do keep it;

I will water it every moment: lest any hurt it,

I will keep it night and day. Fury is not in me:

who would set the briers and thorns against me in battle?

I would go through them, I would burn them together.

Or let him take hold of my strength,

that he may make peace with me;

and he shall make peace with me.

He shall cause them that come of Jacob to take root:

Israel shall blossom and bud,

and fill the face of the world with fruit.

ISAIAH 27:2-6

Ripe blueberries in Maine's
Blueberry Barrens color the
face of the earth.

T|hy mercy, O LORD, is in the heavens;

and thy faithfulness reacheth unto the clouds.

Thy righteousness is like the great mountains;

thy judgments are a great deep:

O LORD, thou preservest man and beast.

How excellent is thy lovingkindness,

O God! therefore the children of men

put their trust under the shadow of thy wings.

They shall be abundantly satisfied with the fatness

of thy house; and thou shalt make them drink

of the river of thy pleasures.

For with thee is the fountain of life:

in thy light shall we see light.

PSALM 36:5-9

Water from New Hampshire's
Lake Winnipesaukee sustains
the nearby trees.

W

hen the Most High divided to the nations

their inheritance, when he separated the sons of Adam, he set the bounds

of the people according to the number of the children of Israel.

For the LORD's portion is his people; Jacob is the lot of his inheritance.

He found him in a desert land, and in the waste howling wilderness; he led him about,

he instructed him, he kept him as the apple of his eye. As an eagle stirreth up her nest,

fluttereth over her young, spreadeth abroad her wings, taketh them,

beareth them on her wings: So the LORD alone did lead him, and there was

no strange god with him. He made him ride on the high places of the earth,

that he might eat the increase of the fields; and he made him to suck honey

out of the rock, and oil out of the flinty rock; Butter of kine, and milk of sheep,

with fat of lambs, and rams of the breed of Bashan, and goats,

with the fat of kidneys of wheat; and thou didst drink the pure blood of the grape.

DEUTERONOMY 32:8-14

An oak tree is strongly rooted
in the lush hills of Vermont.

Fairest Lord Jesus

"Munster Gesangbuch"

Silesian Folk Song

1. Fair - est Lord Je - sus! Ru - ler of all
2. Fair are the mead - ows, Fair - er still the

na - ture, O thou of God and man, the
wood - lands, Robed in the bloom - ing garb of

Son! Thee will I cher - ish, Thee will I
spring: Je - sus is fair - er, Je - sus is

hon - or, Thou, my soul's glo - ry, joy, and crown!
pur - er, Who makes the woe - ful heart to sing.

Fair is the sunshine,

Fairer still the moonlight,

And all the twinkling starry host:

Jesus shines brighter,

Jesus shines purer,

Than all the angels heav'n can boast.

Beautiful Saviour!

Lord of the nations!

Son of God and Son of Man!

Glory and honor,

Praise, adoration,

Now and forevermore be thine!

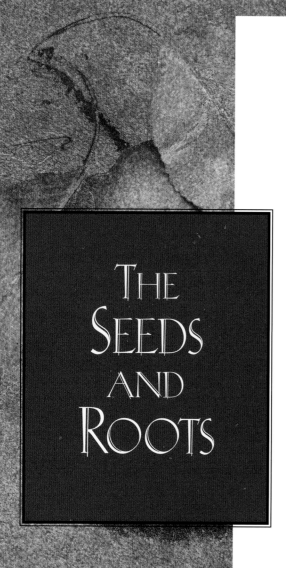

THE SEEDS AND ROOTS

God made the tallest

tree grow from the

tiniest seed and the

invisible root larger

than the plant above.

PLANT A TREE

Lucy Larcom

He who plants a tree
Plants a hope.
Rootlets up through fibres blindly grope;
Leaves unfold into horizons free.
So man's life must climb
From the clods of time
Unto heavens sublime.
Canst thou prophesy, thou little tree,
What the glory of thy boughs shall be?

He who plants a tree
Plants a joy;
Plants a comfort that will never cloy;
Every day a fresh reality,
Beautiful and strong,
To whose shelter throng
Creatures blithe with song.
If thou couldst but know, thou happy tree,
Of the bliss that shall inhabit thee!

He who plants a tree,
He plants love,
Tents of coolness spreading out above
Wayfarers he may not live to see.
Gifts that grow are best;
Hands that bless are blest;
Plant! life does the rest!
Heaven and earth help him who plants a tree,
And his work its own reward shall be.

TREES

Joyce Kilmer

I think that I shall never see
A poem as lovely as a tree.

A tree whose hungry mouth is prest
Against the earth's sweet flowing breast;

A tree that looks at God all day,
And lifts her leafy arms to pray;

A tree that may in Summer wear
A nest of robins in her hair;

Upon whose bosoms snow has lain;
Who intimately lives with rain.

Poems are made by fools like me,
But only God can make a tree.

NOW IS THE HIGH-TIDE OF THE YEAR

James Russell Lowell

Now is the high-tide of the year,
And whatever of life hath ebbed away
Comes flooding back, with a ripply cheer,
Into every bare inlet and creek and bay;
Now the heart is so full that a drop overfills it,
We are happy now because God wills it;
No matter how barren the past may have been,
'Tis enough for us now that the leaves are green;
We sit in the warm shade and feel right well
How the sap creeps up and the blossoms swell;
We may shut our eyes, but we cannot help knowing
That skies are clear and grass is growing;
The breeze comes whispering in our ear,
That dandelions are blossoming near,
That maize has sprouted, that streams are flowing,
That the river is bluer than the sky,
That the robin is plastering his house hard by;
And if the breeze kept the good news back,
For other couriers we should not lack;

We could guess it all by yon heifer's lowing,
And hark! How clear bold chanticleer,
Warmed with the new wine of the year,
Tells all in his lusty crowing!

Joy comes, grief goes, we know not how;
Every thing is happy now,
Every thing is upward striving;
'Tis as easy now for the heart to be true
As for grass to be green or skies to be blue,
'Tis the natural way of living:
Who knows whither the clouds have fled?
In the unscarred heaven they leave no wake,
And the eyes forget the tears they have shed,
The heart forgets its sorrow and ache;
The soul partakes the season's youth,
And the sulphurous rifts of passion and woe
Lie deep 'neath a silence pure and smooth,
Like burnt-out craters healed with snow.

And of Joseph he said, Blessed of the LORD

be his land, for the precious things of heaven, for the dew,

and for the deep that coucheth beneath, And for the precious fruits

brought forth by the sun, and for the precious things put forth

by the moon, And for the chief things of the ancient mountains,

and for the precious things of the lasting hills,

And for the precious things of the earth and fulness thereof,

and for the good will of him that dwelt in the bush:

let the blessing come upon the head of Joseph, and upon the top

of the head of him that was separated from his brethren.

The eternal God is thy refuge, and underneath are the everlasting arms:

and he shall thrust out the enemy from before thee; and shall say,

Destroy them. Israel then shall dwell in safety alone:

the fountain of Jacob shall be upon a land of corn and wine;

also his heavens shall drop down dew.

DEUTERONOMY 33:13-16, 27-28

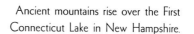

Ancient mountains rise over the First
Connecticut Lake in New Hampshire.

A nd he shewed me a pure river

of water of life, clear as crystal, proceeding out

of the throne of God and of the Lamb. In the midst of the street of it,

and on either side of the river, was there the tree of life,

which bare twelve manner of fruits, and yielded her fruit every month:

and the leaves of the tree were for the healing of the nations.

And there shall be no more curse: but the throne of God

and of the Lamb shall be in it; and his servants shall serve him:

And they shall see his face; and his name shall be in their foreheads.

And there shall be no night there; and they need no candle,

neither light of the sun; for the Lord God giveth them light:

and they shall reign for ever and ever.

REVELATION 22:1-5

Cosby Creek flows through Great Smoky
Mountains National Park and shares its
waters with the trees and creatures.

Then shall he give the rain of thy seed,

that thou shalt sow the ground withal;

and bread of the increase of the earth, and it shall be fat

and plenteous: in that day shall thy cattle feed in large pastures.

The oxen likewise and the young asses that ear the ground

shall eat clean provender, which hath been winnowed

with the shovel and with the fan. And there shall be

upon every high mountain, and upon every high hill,

rivers and streams of waters in the day of the great slaughter,

when the towers fall. Moreover the light of the moon

shall be as the light of the sun, and the light of the sun

shall be sevenfold, as the light of seven days, in the day

that the LORD bindeth up the breach of his people,

and healeth the stroke of their wound.

ISAIAH 30:23-26

Under a blue sky, a field of golden
grain waits for the harvest.

By terrible things in righteousness wilt thou answer us,

O God of our salvation; who art the confidence of all the ends of the earth,

and of them that are afar off upon the sea: Which by his strength setteth fast

the mountains; being girded with power: Which stilleth the noise of the seas,

the noise of their waves, and the tumult of the people.

They also that dwell in the uttermost parts are afraid at thy tokens:

thou makest the outgoings of the morning and evening to rejoice.

Thou visitest the earth, and waterest it: thou greatly enrichest it with the river of God,

which is full of water: thou preparest them corn, when thou hast so provided for it.

Thou waterest the ridges thereof abundantly: thou settlest the furrows thereof:

thou makest it soft with showers: thou blessest the springing thereof.

Thou crownest the year with thy goodness; and thy paths drop fatness.

They drop upon the pastures of the wilderness: and the little hills rejoice on every side.

The pastures are clothed with flocks; the valleys also are covered over with corn;

they shout for joy, they also sing.

PSALM 65:5-13

A Time for All Seasons

Chapter 5

Snow and ice blanket the earth
during the restful season of winter.

T o every thing there is a season,

and a time to every purpose under the heaven:

A time to be born, and a time to die; a time to plant,

and a time to pluck up that which is planted; A time to kill,

and a time to heal; a time to break down, and a time to build up;

A time to weep, and a time to laugh; a time to mourn,

and a time to dance; A time to cast away stones,

and a time to gather stones together; a time to embrace,

and a time to refrain from embracing; A time to get,

and a time to lose; a time to keep, and a time to cast away;

A time to rend, and a time to sew; a time to keep silence,

and a time to speak; A time to love, and a time to hate;

a time of war, and a time of peace.

ECCLESIASTES 3:1-8

Birches and maples turn
colors in the autumn as the
earth prepares for winter.

M

y beloved spake, and said unto me,

Rise up, my love, my fair one, and come away.

For, lo, the winter is past, the rain is over and gone;

The flowers appear on the earth;

the time of the singing of birds is come,

and the voice of the turtle is heard in our land;

The fig tree putteth forth her green figs,

and the vines with the tender grape give a good smell.

Arise, my love, my fair one, and come away.

SONG OF SOLOMON 2:10-13

New leaves dance on the live oak trees
at Oak Alley Plantation in Louisiana.

Hast thou entered into the treasures of the snow?

or hast thou seen the treasures of the hail, Which I have reserved

against the time of trouble, against the day of battle and war?

By what way is the light parted, which scattereth the east wind upon the earth?

Who hath divided a watercourse for the overflowing of waters,

or a way for the lightning of thunder; To cause it to rain on the earth,

where no man is; on the wilderness, wherein there is no man;

To satisfy the desolate and waste ground; and to cause the bud

of the tender herb to spring forth? Hath the rain a father?

or who hath begotten the drops of dew? Out of whose womb came the ice?

and the hoary frost of heaven, who hath gendered it?

The waters are hid as with a stone, and the face of the deep is frozen.

JOB 38:22-30

The treasures of snow dot the
Smith River in New Hampshire.

LET ALL THINGS NOW LIVING

Katherine K. Davis

Welsh Melody

1. Let all things now liv-ing A song of thanks-
2. His law he en-forc-es; The stars in their

giv-ing To God the Cre-a-tor tri-um-phant-ly
cours-es And sun in its or-bit o-be-dient-ly

raise; Who fash-ioned and made us, Pro-tect-ed and
shine. The hills and the moun-tains, The riv-ers and

stayed us, Who still guides us on to the end of our
foun-tains, The deeps of the o-cean pro-claim him di-

days. God's ban-ners are o'er us; His light goes be -
vine. We too should be voic-ing Our love and re -

fore us— A pil-lar of fire shin-ing forth in the
joic-ing, With glad ad - o - ra-tion a song let us

night— Till shad-ows have van-ished and dark-ness is
raise Till all things now liv - ing u - nite in thanks -

ban-ished, As for-ward we trav-el from light in-to light.
giv-ing: "To God in the high-est, ho-san-na and praise!"

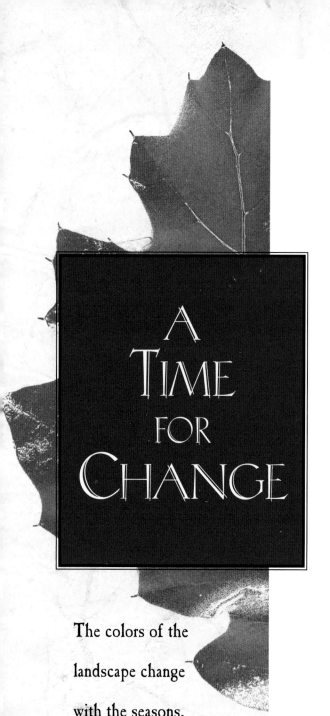

A Time for Change

The colors of the

landscape change

with the seasons.

THE SNOWSTORM

Ralph Waldo Emerson

Announced by all the trumpets of the sky,
Arrives the snow, and, driving o'er the fields,
Seems nowhere to alight: the whited air
Hides hill and woods, the river, and the heaven,
And veils the farmhouse at the garden's end.
The sled and traveller stopped, the courier's feet
Delayed, all friends shut out, the housemates sit
Around the radiant fireplace, enclosed
In a tumultuous privacy of storm.

Come, see the north wind's masonry.
Out of an unseen quarry evermore
Furnished with tile, the fierce artificer
Curves his white bastions with projected roof
Round every windward stake or tree or door.
Speeding, the myriad-handed, his wild work
So fanciful, so savage, naught cares he
For number or proportion. Mockingly,
On coop or kennel he hangs Parian wreaths;
A swan-like form invests the hiddden thorn;
Fills up the famer's lane from wall to wall,
Maugre the farmer's sighs; and at the gate
A tapering turret overtops the work.
And when his hours are numbered, and the world
Is all his own, retiring, as he were not,
Leaves, when the sun appears, astonished Art
To mimic in slow structures, stone by stone,
Built in an age, the mad wind's night-work,
The frolic architecture of the snow.

To Autumn

John Keats

Season of mists and mellow fruitfulness,
Close bosom-friend of the maturing sun;
Conspiring with him how to load and bless
With fruit the vines that round the thatch-eves run;
To bend with apples the moss'd cottage-trees,
And fill all fruit with ripeness to the core;
To swell the gourd, and plump the hazel shells
With a sweet kernel; to set budding more,
And still more, later flowers for the bees,
Until they think warm days will never cease,
For Summer has o'er-brimm'd their clammy cells.

Who hath not seen thee oft amid thy store?
Sometimes whoever seeks abroad may find
Thee sitting careless on a granary floor,
Thy hair soft-lifted by the winnowing wind;
Or on a half-reap'd furrow sound asleep,
Drows'd with the fume of poppies, while thy hook

Spares the next swath and all its twinèd flowers:
And sometimes like a gleaner thou dost keep
Steady thy laden head across a brook;
Or by a cyder-press, with patient look,
Thou watchest the last oozings hours by hours.

Where are the songs of Spring? Ay, where are they?
Think not of them, thou hast thy music too,
While barred clouds bloom the soft-dying day,
And touch the stubble plains with rosy hue;
Then in a wailful choir the small gnats mourn
Among the river sallows, borne aloft
Or sinking as the light wind lives or dies;
And full-grown lambs loud bleat from hilly bourn;
Hedge-crickets sing; and now with treble soft
The red-breast whistles from a garden-croft;
And gathering swallows twitter in the skies.

Written at the Close of Spring

Charlotte Smith

The garlands fade that Spring so lately wove,
Each simple flower, which she had nurs'd in dew,
Anemonies that spangled every grove,
The primrose wan, and hare-bell, mildly blue.
No more shall violets linger in the dell,
Or purple orchis variegate the plain,
Till Spring again shall call forth every bell,

And dress with humid hands her wreaths again—
Ah! poor humanity! so frail, so fair,
Are the fond visions of thy early day,
Till tyrant passion, and corrosive care,
Bid all thy fairy colours fade away!
Another May new buds and flowers shall bring;
Ah! why has happiness—no second Spring?

At this also my heart trembleth, and is moved

out of his place. Hear attentively the noise of his voice,

and the sound that goeth out of his mouth. He directeth it under the whole heaven,

and his lightning unto the ends of the earth. After it a voice roareth:

he thundereth with the voice of his excellency; and he will not stay them

when his voice is heard. God thundereth marvellously with his voice;

great things doeth he, which we cannot comprehend. For he saith to the snow,

Be thou on the earth; likewise to the small rain, and to the great rain of his strength.

He sealeth up the hand of every man; that all men may know his work.

Then the beasts go into dens, and remain in their places.

Out of the south cometh the whirlwind: and cold out of the north.

By the breath of God frost is given: and the breadth of the waters is straitened.

Also by watering he wearieth the thick cloud: he scattereth his bright cloud:

And it is turned round about by his counsels: that they may do whatsoever

he commandeth them upon the face of the world in the earth.

JOB 37:1-12

The glorious hues of black-eyed
Susans brighten a field of wildflowers.

And the LORD said in his heart, I will not again

curse the ground any more for man's sake; for the imagination

of man's heart is evil from his youth; neither will I again smite any more

every thing living, as I have done. While the earth remaineth, seedtime and harvest,

and cold and heat, and summer and winter, and day and night shall not cease.

And God said, This is the token of the covenant which I make between me and you

and every living creature that is with you, for perpetual generations:

I do set my bow in the cloud, and it shall be for a token of a covenant between

me and the earth. And it shall come to pass, when I bring a cloud over the earth,

that the bow shall be seen in the cloud: And I will remember my covenant,

which is between me and you and every living creature of all flesh;

and the waters shall no more become a flood to destroy all flesh. And the bow

shall be in the cloud; and I will look upon it, that I may remember the everlasting

covenant between God and every living creature of all flesh that is upon the earth.

And God said unto Noah, This is the token of the covenant,

which I have established between me and all flesh that is upon the earth.

GENESIS 8:21B-22; 9:12-17

A rainbow arches over Mount Prospect
and Mount Fitch in Pisgah National Forest.

For, behold, I create new heavens and a new earth:

and the former shall not be remembered, nor come into mind. But be ye glad

and rejoice for ever in that which I create: for, behold, I create Jerusalem a rejoicing,

and her people a joy. And I will rejoice in Jerusalem, and joy in my people:

and the voice of weeping shall be no more heard in her, nor the voice of crying.

And they shall build houses, and inhabit them; and they shall plant vineyards,

and eat the fruit of them. They shall not build, and another inhabit;

they shall not plant, and another eat: for as the days of a tree are the days

of my people, and mine elect shall long enjoy the work of their hands.

They shall not labour in vain, nor bring forth for trouble;

for they are the seed of the blessed of the LORD, and their offspring with them.

And it shall come to pass, that before they call, I will answer; and while

they are yet speaking, I will hear. The wolf and the lamb shall feed together,

and the lion shall eat straw like the bullock: and dust shall be the serpent's meat.

They shall not hurt nor destroy in all my holy mountain, saith the LORD.

ISAIAH 65:17-19, 21-25

In Pisgah National Forest, the rhododendrons
blossom amidst the spruce trees.

Hallelujah, Praise Jehovah

Psalm 148

William J. Kirkpatrick

1. Hal - le - lu - jah, praise Je - ho - vah, from the
2. Let them prais - es give Je - ho - vah, they were

heav - ens praise his name; Praise Je - ho - vah in the
made at his com - mand; Them for - ev - er he es -

high - est, all his an - gels, praise pro - claim. All his
tab - lished, his de - cree shall ev - er stand, From the

hosts, to - geth - er praise him, sun and moon and stars on high; Praise him,
earth, O praise Je - ho - vah, all you seas, you mon - sters all, Fire and

O you heav'ns of   heav - ens, and you floods a - bove the   sky.
hail and snow and   va - pors, storm - y   winds that hear his   call.

Refrain:

Let them prais - es give Je - ho - vah, for his
Let   them   prais - es

name a - lone is   high,   And his glo - ry is ex -
And his glo - ry

alt - ed, and his glo - ry is ex - alt - ed, And his
and   his   glo - ry

glo - ry is ex - alt - ed far a - bove the earth and   sky.
and his glo - ry

A Time of Growth

Underneath the

snow, the bud

waits for the time

when it will bloom.

A Winter Walk

John Clare

The holly bush, a sober lump of green,
Shines through the leafless shrubs all brown and grey,
And smiles at winter, be it e'er so keen,
With all the leafy luxury of May.
And oh, it is delicious, when the day
In winter's loaded garment keenly blows
And turns her back on sudden falling snows,
To go where gravel pathways creep between
Arches of evergreen that scarce let through
A single feather of the driving storm;
And in the bitterest day that ever blew
The walk will find some places still and warm
Where dead leaves rustle sweet and give alarm
To little birds that flirt and start away.

Winter

Robert Southey

A wrinkled crabbed man they picture thee,
Old Winter, with a rugged beard as grey
As the long moss upon the apple-tree;
Blue-lipt, an ice-drop at thy sharp blue nose,
Close muffled up, and on thy dreary way
Plodding alone through sleet and drifting snows.
They should have drawn thee by the high-heapt hearth,
Old Winter! seated in thy great armed chair,
Watching the children at their Christmas mirth;
Or circled by them as thy lips declare
Some merry jest, or tale of murder dire,
Or troubled spirit that disturbs the night,
Pausing at times to rouse the mouldering fire,
Or taste the old October brown and bright.

To Spring

William Blake

O thou, with dewy locks, who lookest down
Thro' the clear windows of the morning; turn
Thine angel eyes upon our western isle,
Which in full choir hails thy approach, O Spring!

The hills tell each other, and the list'ning
Vallies hear; all our longing eyes are turned
Up to thy bright pavilions: issue forth,
And let thy holy feet visit our clime.

Come o'er the eastern hills, and let our winds
Kiss thy perfumed garments; let us taste
Thy morn and evening breath; scatter thy pearls
Upon our love-sick land that mourns for thee.

O deck her forth with thy fair fingers; pour
Thy soft kisses on her bosom; and put
Thy golden crown upon her languish'd head,
Whose modest tresses were bound up for thee!

To Summer

William Blake

O thou, who passest thro' our vallies in
Thy strength, curb thy fierce steeds, allay the heat
That flames from their large nostrils! thou, O Summer,
Oft pitched'st here thy golden tent, and oft
Beneath our oaks hast slept, while we beheld
With joy thy ruddy limbs and flourishing hair.

Beneath our thickest shades we oft have heard
Thy voice, when noon upon his fervid car
Rode o'er the deep of heaven; beside our springs
Sit down, and in our mossy vallies, on
Some bank beside a river clear, throw thy
Silk draperies off, and rush into the stream:
Our vallies love the Summer in his pride.

Our bards are fam'd who strike the silver wire:
Our youths are bolder than the southern swains:
Our maidens fairer in the sprightly dance:
We lack not songs, nor instruments of joy,
Nor echoes sweet, nor waters clear as heaven,
Nor laurel wreaths against the sultry heat.

To Autumn

William Blake

O Autumn, laden with fruit, and stained
With the blood of the grape, pass not, but sit
Beneath my shady roof; there thou may'st rest,
And tune thy jolly voice to my fresh pipe;
And all the daughters of the year shall dance!
Sing now the lusty song of fruits and flowers.

"The narrow bud opens her beauties to
The sun, and love runs in her thrilling veins;
Blossoms hang round the brows of morning, and
Flourish down the bright cheek of modest eve,
Till clustr'ing Summer breaks forth into singing,
And feather'd clouds strew flowers round her head."

"The spirits of the air live on the smells
Of fruit; and joy, with pinions light, roves round
The gardens, or sits singing in the trees."
Thus sang the jolly Autumn as he sat;
Then rose, girded himself, and o'er the bleak
Hills fled from our sight; but left his golden load.

And God said, Let there be lights

in the firmament of the heaven to divide the day from the night;

and let them be for signs, and for seasons, and for days, and years:

And let them be for lights in the firmament of the heaven

to give light upon the earth: and it was so.

And God made two great lights; the greater light to rule the day,

and the lesser light to rule the night: he made the stars also.

And God set them in the firmament of the heaven to give light

upon the earth, And to rule over the day and over the night,

and to divide the light from the darkness:

and God saw that it was good.

GENESIS 1:14-18

The changing colors of the leaves
are a sign of the season in the
hardwood forest along the banks of
New Hampshire's Warner River.

Thus saith the LORD, In an acceptable time

have I heard thee, and in a day of salvation have I helped thee:

and I will preserve thee, and give thee for a covenant of the people,

to establish the earth, to cause to inherit the desolate heritages;

That thou mayest say to the prisoners, Go forth;

to them that are in darkness, Shew yourselves.

They shall feed in the ways, and their pastures shall be in all high places.

They shall not hunger nor thirst; neither shall the heat nor sun

smite them: for he that hath mercy on them shall lead them,

even by the springs of water shall he guide them. And I will make

all my mountains a way, and my highways shall be exalted.

Sing, O heavens; and be joyful, O earth; and break forth into singing,

O mountains: for the LORD hath comforted his people,

and will have mercy upon his afflicted.

ISAIAH 49:8-11, 13

The light breaks through the trees next
to Hood Pond in Massachusetts.

Sing unto the LORD with thanksgiving;

sing praise upon the harp unto our God:

Who covereth the heaven with clouds,

who prepareth rain for the earth,

who maketh grass to grow upon the mountains.

He giveth to the beast his food,

and to the young ravens which cry.

The eyes of all wait upon thee;

and thou givest them their meat in due season.

Thou openest thine hand,

and satisfiest the desire of every living thing.

PSALM 147:7-9; 145:15-16

Cosby Creek winds through
moss-covered rocks in Great
Smoky Mountains National Park.

Index